Theme 3

D1489096

HOUGHTON MIFFLIN
Reading

Let's Look Around!

HOUGHTON MIFFLIN

BOSTON

Printed in China

ISBN-13: 978-0-618-38711-3

ISBN-10: 0-618-38711-0

6 7 8 9-SDP-08 07 06

Design, Art Management, and Page Production: Studio Goodwin Sturges

Contents

Cabs, Cabs, Cabs

by Wayne Mazzola
illustrated by Robert de Michiell

Mack has a big tan cab.

Mack can pass two big cabs.

The big tan cab hit a big tack.

Mack has to quit.

Fall Naps

by Kelly Teele
illustrated by Lydia Dabcovich

It can get cold.

Dad, Sam, and Jack
pass dens.

An animal can get set to
nap, nap, nap.

Tap, tap, tap.
Birds can get bugs.
Tap, tap, tap.

Pam Can Pack

by Ruth Kwan
illustrated by Linda Wingerter

Look at Pam.

Pam has a big tan sack.

Pam can pack the big
tan sack full.

Pam can get ten big jugs
of big, big flowers.

Lots of Picking

by Kelly Teele

illustrated by Lars Leetaru

Kim is picking.

Kim's Dad picks, too.

Kim can get lots.

Kim's Dad gets lots, too.

They filled big bins.

Bill Bird

by Jason Weeks
illustrated by Enrique O. Sánchez

Bill Bird can eat lots.

First Bill gets six of Jill's nuts.

Bill is picking big, big figs.
Bill will not quit.

Bill picked lots of figs and nuts!

Tim's Cat

by Virginia Houston
illustrated by Anna Alter

Tim's cat is Miss Hiss.

Why is his cat
called Miss Hiss?

Look at Miss Hiss
hissing at the paper!

But Miss Hiss has
never hissed at Tim!

Let's Trim
the Track!

by Rafael Lopez
illustrated by Stacey Schuett

Let's trim the grass
at the track.

Fran can cut the grass.

Gran grabs big bags.

Sam can fit the bags
in the big tan van.

Brad's Quick Rag Tricks

by Diane Patek
illustrated by Lizzy Rockwell

Brad can do quick rag tricks.

Brad picks Gran.
Gran can get a big,
big green rag.

Let's look!
The big rag's brown.

Brad did a quick trick!

Fran Pig's Brick Hut

by Mark Dempsey

illustrated by Amy Walrod

Fran Pig got some
big, fat bricks.

Fran Pig also got many pigs
to grab big, fat bricks.

The pigs set lots
of big, fat bricks.

It's set!

Fran Pig likes the big brick hut.

Word Lists

Cabs, Cabs, Cabs (p. 5) accompanies *Seasons.*

DECODABLE WORDS

Target Skills
Double final consonants:
pass

Final consonants:
cabs, has, Mack, tack

Short *a:*
cab, cabs, can, has, Mack, pass, tack, tan

Plurals with *-s:*
cabs

Words Using Previously Taught Skills
big, hit, quit

HIGH-FREQUENCY WORDS

Previously Taught
a, the, to, two

Fall Naps (p. 9) accompanies *Seasons.*

DECODABLE WORDS

Target Skills
Double final consonants:
pass

Final consonants:
bugs, dens, Jack

Short *a:*
an, can, Dad, Jack, nap, naps, pass, Sam, tap

Plurals with *-s:*
bugs, dens, naps

Words Using Previously Taught Skills
bugs, get, it, set

HIGH-FREQUENCY WORDS

New
animal, birds, cold, fall

Previously Taught
and, to

Theme 3, Week 1

Pam Can Pack (p. 13) accompanies *Seasons.*

DECODABLE WORDS

Target Skills
Final consonants:
has, jugs, pack, sack

Short *a:*
at, can, has, pack, Pam, sack, tan

Plurals with -*s:*
jugs

Words Using Previously Taught Sills
big, get, ten

HIGH-FREQUENCY WORDS

New
flowers, full, look, of

Previously Taught
a, the

Theme 3, Week 2

Lots of Picking (p. 17) accompanies *Miss Jill's Ice Cream Shop.*

DECODABLE WORDS

Target Skills

Verb Endings *-s, -ed, -ing:*
gets, picks, filled, picking

Short *i:*
big, bins, filled, Kim's, Kim, picking, picks

Possessives *('s):*
Kim's

Words Using Previously Taught Skills
can, Dad, get, lots

HIGH-FREQUENCY WORDS

Previously Taught
is, of, they, too

Theme 3, Week 2

Bill Bird (p. 21) accompanies *Miss Jill's Ice Cream Shop.*

DECODABLE WORDS

Target Skills

Verb Endings *-s, -ed, -ing:*
gets, picked, picking

Short *i:*
big, Bill, fig, figs, Jill's, picked, picking, quit, six, will

Possessives *('s):*
Jill's

Words Using Previously Taught Skills
can, lots, nuts, six

HIGH-FREQUENCY WORDS

New
eat, first

Previously Taught
bird, is, not, of

43

Theme 3, Week 2

Tim's Cat (p. 25) accompanies *Miss Jill's Ice Cream Shop.*

DECODABLE WORDS

Target Skills
Verb Endings -*s*, -*ed*, -*ing*:
hissed, hissing

Short *i*:
his, Hiss, hissed, hissing, Miss, Tim, Tim's

Possessives *('s)*:
Tim's

Words Using Previously Taught Skills
at, but, cat, has, Tim

HIGH-FREQUENCY WORDS

New
called, never, paper, why

Previously Taught
is, look, the

Theme 3, Week 3

Let's Trim the Track! (p. 29) accompanies *At the Aquarium.*

DECODABLE WORDS

Target Skills
Consonant Clusters with *r*:
Fran, grabs, Gran, grass, track, trim

Contractions with -*'s*:
Let's

Words Using Previously Taught Skills
at, bags, big, can, cut, fit, Sam, tan, van

HIGH-FREQUENCY WORDS

Previously Taught
in, the

Theme 3, Week 3

Brad's Quick Rag Tricks (p. 33) accompanies *At the Aquarium.*

DECODABLE WORDS

Target Skills

Consonant Clusters with *r:*
Brad, Brad's, Gran, tricks

Contractions with -*'s:*
Let's, rag's

Words Using Previously Taught Skills
big, can, did, get, picks, quick, rag

HIGH-FREQUENCY WORDS

New
brown, green

Previously Taught
a, do, look, the

Theme 3, Week 3

Fran Pig's Brick Hut (p. 37) accompanies *At the Aquarium.*

DECODABLE WORDS

Target Skills

Consonant Clusters with *r:*
brick, bricks, Fran, grab

Contractions with -*'s:*
it's

Words Using Previously Taught Skills
big, fat, got, hut, lots, pig, pig's, pigs, set

HIGH-FREQUENCY WORDS

New
also, likes, many, some

Previously Taught
of, the, to

45

HIGH-FREQUENCY WORDS TAUGHT TO DATE

a	call	five	here	my	see	what
all	cold	flower	I	never	shall	where
also	color	for	in	not	some	who
and	do	four	is	of	they	why
animal	does	full	jump	on	three	you
are	eat	funny	like	once	to	
away	every	go	live	one	too	
bird	fall	green	look	paper	two	
blue	find	have	many	pull	upon	
brown	first	he	me	said	we	

Decoding skills taught to date: Consonants *m, s, t, c,* consonants *n, f, p,* short *a,* consonants *b, r, h, g,* short *i,* consonants *d, w, l, x,* short *o,* consonants *y, k, v,* short *e,* consonants *q, j, z,* short *u,* double final consonants, final consonants, plurals with *-s,* verb endings *-s, -ed, -ing,* possessives, consonant clusters with *r,* contractions with *-'s*

46